Super Simple
STEAM
Activities

REBECCA FELIX

Lerner Publications ◆ Minneapolis

Official Licensed Product
Lerner Publications Company
An imprint of Lerner Publishing Group, Inc.
241 First Avenue North
Minneapolis, MN 55401 USA

For reading levels and more information, look up this title at www.lernerbooks.com.

Main body text set in Syntax LT Std
Typeface provided by Adobe

Library of Congress Cataloging-in-Publication Data

Names: Felix, Rebecca, 1984– author.
Title: Crayola super simple STEAM activities / Rebecca Felix.
Description: Minneapolis : Lerner Publications, [2022] | Series: Crayola makers | Includes bibliographical references and index. | Audience: Ages 8–11 | Audience: Grades 2–3 | Summary: "Use everyday materials to explore STEAM principles: build a maze from paper plates and chenille stems, create collages with overlapping mediums, make a mosaic out of clay, and explore tessellations by remixing art"— Provided by publisher.
Identifiers: LCCN 2020045445 (print) | LCCN 2020045446 (ebook) | ISBN 9781728403205 (library binding) | ISBN 9781728417875 (ebook)
Subjects: LCSH: Science—Experiments—Juvenile literature. | Science projects—Juvenile literature. | Handicraft for children—Juvenile literature.
Classification: LCC Q164 .F3535 2022 (print) | LCC Q164 (ebook) | DDC 745.59—dc23

LC record available at https://lccn.loc.gov/2020045445
LC ebook record available at https://lccn.loc.gov/2020045446

Manufactured in the United States of America
2-51705-48835-9/1/2021

TABLE OF CONTENTS

STEAM Means...

STEAM holds many amazing things in just five letters! Each letter stands for a different discipline. These are science, technology, engineering, arts, and math.

STEAM is all around you, everywhere you go! Art supplies are one example. The sciences of color and chemistry are used to create different hues and mediums. Manufacturers use technology to make art tools. Engineers design different paintbrushes, markers, and other art products. Math ensures that all pieces in sets have the same dimensions, such as the crayons in a box. Then people use these supplies to make art!

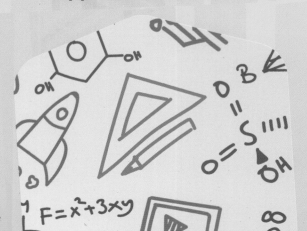

Simple STEAM

Exploring STEAM is simple! Use everyday materials to explore sound, make a maze, remix art, and more.

STEAM Safety

Some projects require the use of heat, sharp tools, or substances that can be unsafe if misused. Follow these rules to explore STEAM safely:

- Ask an adult for permission and help before using heat or sharp tools.

- Do not touch your eyes, nose, or mouth during a STEAM project.

- Wash your hands after using glues, dyes, and paints.

- Read and follow all instructions that come with any product you use.

Stormy Sea in a Bottle

Make waves and learn why some liquids won't mix.

Materials:

recycled plastic water or soda bottle with cap, paint, paintbrushes, canola or vegetable oil, liquid measuring cup, water, blue food coloring, spoon

1 Peel any labels from the plastic bottle. Set the bottle on its side. Paint storm clouds on the side of the bottle.

2 Stand the bottle upright. Fill it halfway with oil. Wait a few minutes for the oil to settle.

3 Measure 1 cup (236 mL) of water. Stir in five to six drops of food coloring.

4 Slowly pour the colored water into the bottle. Watch what happens! Water is denser than oil, so it will move to the bottom.

5 Screw the bottle's cap on tightly. Turn the bottle on its side. Gently rock the bottle to make waves.

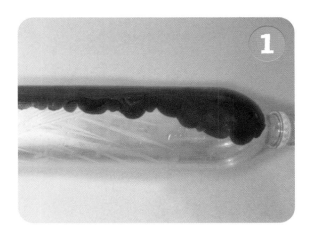

STEAM Takeaway

Water molecules are polar. Oil molecules are nonpolar. Polar and nonpolar molecules cannot mix together. Food coloring molecules are polar, so they mix with water. Neither water nor food coloring mixes with oil. Also, oil is less dense than water. So, it floats on top of the water.

Form Sculpture

Materials:

recycled objects that are different forms: paper towel tube (cylinder), small box (cube), small, lightweight ball (sphere); air-dry clay; cardboard; paper; scissors; tape; school glue; rubber bands; paint; paintbrushes; decorations

Transform geometric forms into a 3D work of art.

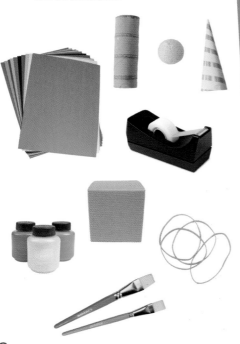

1. Search for small objects at home that are geometric forms. Look for spheres, cylinders, pyramids, cubes, cones, and prisms. Gather as many as possible. Get adult permission to use the objects.

2. Examine the objects. Think about how they could be used to make a sculpture. Which seem best suited for the sculpture's base? Which should be placed higher up? What materials could you use to connect the objects?

3. Test your ideas. As you experiment, think about what forms you could use more of. Try creating these forms out of materials such as clay, cardboard, or paper.

4. Build a sculpture using the objects you gathered and the forms you created. Use tape, glue, rubber bands, or other materials to connect the forms.

5. Paint or decorate your sculpture. Then display your geometric art!

Hubble Space Portrait

Create celestial paintings inspired by real space photos!

Materials:

tablet or computer, tempera paint, glitter glue, paintbrushes, plastic plate, paper towel, plastic mat, sponges, bowl of water, black construction paper, bowl, pencil, scissors, metallic markers, school glue

1 Have an adult help you search online for photos taken by the Hubble Space Telescope. Study the photos to see what galaxies and stars look like.

2 Mix different colors of paint and glitter glue on the plastic plate.

3 Place the paper towel on the plastic mat. Dip a sponge in the water and then the paint and glue. Dab the sponge on the paper towel. Make patterns that look like galaxies and stars.

4 Let the paper towel dry overnight.

5 Place a bowl upside down in the center of a sheet of black construction paper. Trace around the bowl. Cut out the circle to make a round hole like the telescope's lens.

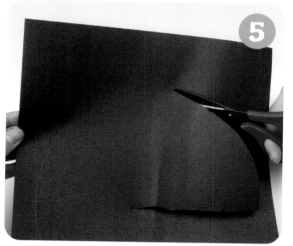

6 Use metallic markers to draw lens details on the paper.

7 Glue the construction paper to the paper towel to frame your space art. Cut off any paper towel that sticks out past the construction paper.

STEAM Takeaway

The Hubble Space Telescope orbits Earth. It takes photos of stars, planets, and galaxies. This includes Earth's galaxy, the Milky Way. Scientists think there could be as many as two trillion galaxies in the universe.

Mosaic Puzzle

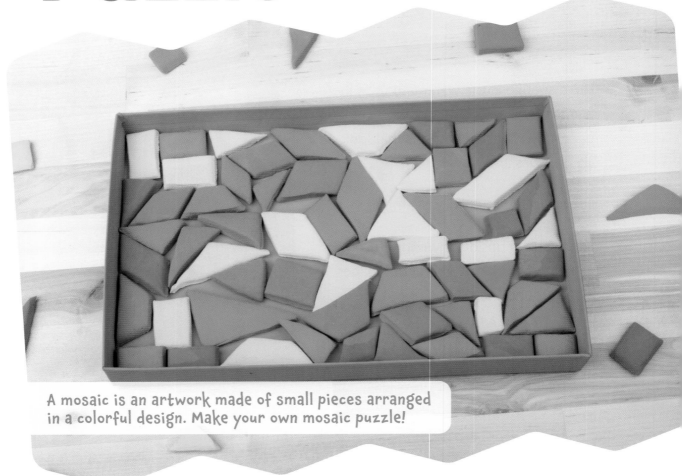

A mosaic is an artwork made of small pieces arranged in a colorful design. Make your own mosaic puzzle!

Materials:

Model Magic in several colors, rolling pin, ruler, plastic knife, paint, paintbrushes, shoebox lid, school glue (optional)

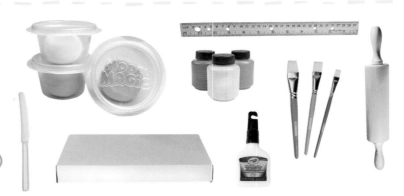

1 Roll out each color of clay until it is about 1 inch (2.5 cm) thick.

2 Cut the clay into about twenty-five small geometric shapes.

3 Paint the shoebox lid.

4 Let the clay pieces and the paint dry.

5 Fit the clay pieces into the shoebox lid. Arrange them in different mosaic designs.

6 If you create a mosaic you want to keep, glue the pieces in place on the lid. Or, leave the pieces loose and design with them again and again!

Ever-Changing Maze

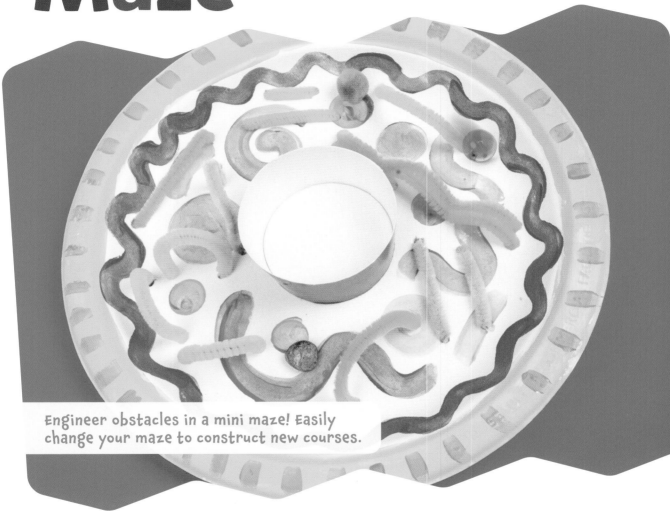

Engineer obstacles in a mini maze! Easily change your maze to construct new courses.

Materials:

paper cup, scissors, sturdy paper plate, school glue, hole punch, paint, paintbrushes, chenille stems, marble, pom-pom, pebble

1 Cut off the top two-thirds of the cup. Glue the bottom of the cup to the center of the plate.

2 Randomly punch holes into the plate around the cup.

3 Paint the plate and cup however you like. Let the paint dry.

4 Cut chenille stems of different lengths. Weave them through the punched holes. Create tunnels, bridges, ramps, and paths. Twist the ends of the stems together under the plate to keep them in place.

5 Place the marble, pom-pom, and pebble in the cup. Your maze is ready!

6 Take the marble from the cup and set it on the plate. Tip the plate in different directions to roll the marble through the maze.

7 Try the pom-pom next, and then the pebble. How well did each object travel? Why? Think about the objects' weights and shapes. Do these things affect their ability to move through the maze?

8 Move the chenille stems to change your maze again and again! Can you engineer the maze to help the objects move through it more quickly?

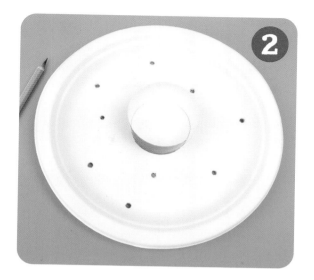

Tessellation Masterpiece

Use an orderly geometry concept to transform an image into your own art!

Materials:

tablet or computer, printer, ruler, pencil, scissors, card stock, tape, school glue, construction paper

1. Have an adult help you search online for a colorful photograph or artwork. Print the image. Size it to take up as much of the paper as possible. Cut off the white edges around the image.

2. Cut the image into nine rectangles. Make sure they are all the same size. Trace one of the rectangles on card stock. Cut it out.

3. Draw a line across the card stock rectangle. It can be any shape. It just needs to start in one corner and end in another corner. Cut along the line to cut the rectangle into two pieces.

4. Place one of the card stock pieces on the back of a paper rectangle. Trace around the card stock shape. Repeat with all paper rectangles.

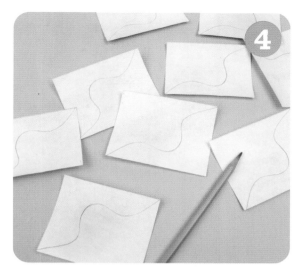

5. Cut along the line on one paper rectangle. Tape the straight sides of the two pieces together. Repeat for all rectangles.

6. Turn the shapes over. Arrange them so they fit together without any gaps or overlaps. Try different arrangements until you find a pattern you like.

7. Glue the shapes to a sheet of construction paper in the pattern you arranged. Leave a border as a frame.

STEAM Takeaway

A tessellation is a pattern of shapes fitted together to cover a flat surface without any overlaps or gaps. Tessellations can often be seen in the world around us, such as in tiled floors and brick paths.

Smartphone Speaker Stand

Design an acoustic speaker that increases your smartphone's volume!

Materials:

notebook, pencil, construction paper, tape, smartphone, scissors, air-dry clay, decorating materials

1. Draw a plan to create a tube out of construction paper and tape. Think about how to make the paper as stiff as possible. Would using several layers work? Or covering the paper with tape?

2. Design a way for a smartphone's speaker to rest inside the tube. The tube should also act as a stand for the device. Would cutting a slot into the tube work? How about adding a clay base to hold the tube in place?

3. Construct your speaker stand. Place the smartphone inside. Does the stand support it? If the stand falls over, think about how to fix it. This could mean using more clay or adding legs. Changing the tube to hold the phone at a different angle might help too.

4. Once the stand can hold the phone, play music or other sounds to test the speaker. Does the stand increase the phone's volume? If not, brainstorm why. Are there any small tears in the tube where sound is escaping? Did the tube get bent or crumpled? A smooth inner surface works best.

5. When your speaker stand is complete and working, paint or decorate it. When everything is dry, place your phone in it. Enjoy your favorite song or other audio with enhanced sound!

STEAM Takeaway

Acoustics is how different spaces and surfaces affect sound. Sound waves from your phone vibrate against the sides of the tube. The hollow tube makes the sounds louder. Acoustic instruments, such as guitars, have hollow bodies that work the same way to produce music when their strings vibrate.

Full Moon Illusion

Watch two moon phases merge into a full moon in a glowing optical illusion!

Materials:

tablet or computer, pencil with eraser, notebook, plastic cup, 2 unruled index cards, ruler, colored pencils, glow-in-the-dark paint, tape

1 Have an adult help you research moon phases online. Draw the moon's phases in a circle in a notebook. Make sure they are in the correct order. Label each phase.

2 With a pencil, lightly trace the bottom of the cup on each index card. Measure to make sure the circles are in the centers of the cards.

3 Look at the moon phases you drew. Choose any two phases directly across from each other, except the new moon and full moon. Color each chosen phase inside one traced circle. Erase the rest of the circle lines.

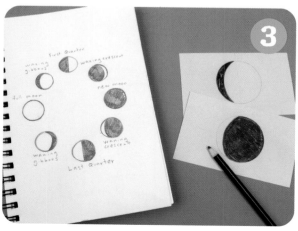

Project continued on next page.

4 Use colored pencils to draw a night sky around each moon.

5 Paint each moon with glow-in-the-dark paint. Let the paint dry.

6 Tape the end of a pencil to the back of one of the moon drawings.

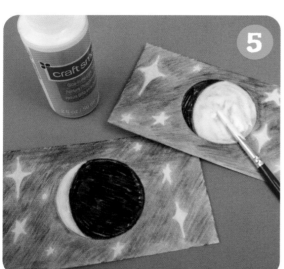

7 Tape the back of the second drawing to the back of the first drawing. The pencil should be between the drawings.

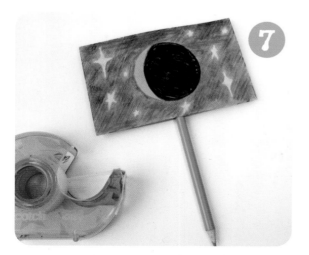

STEAM
Takeaway

The human eye sees an image and sends the information to the brain. This takes a fraction of a second. If the retina sees another image before this fraction of a second ends, the images merge into one! This helps us see motion smoothly.

8 Hold the colored pencil between your palms. Quickly rub your hands together to spin the pencil and drawings. What do you see? What happens to the moon images?

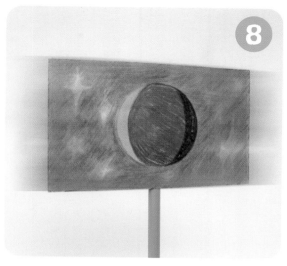

9 Try spinning the drawings again. Look at the them while blinking your eyes rapidly. Does this affect what you see?

10 Go into a dark room and spin the drawings again. Now what do they look like?

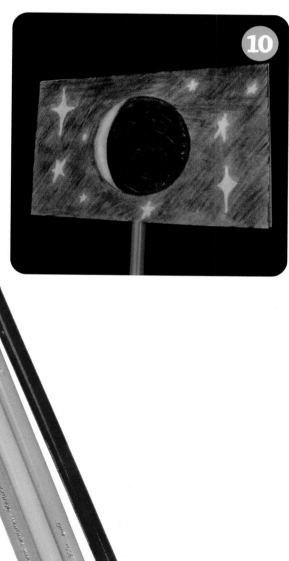

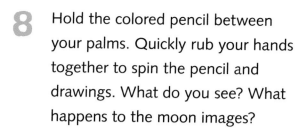

Mini da Vinci Bridge

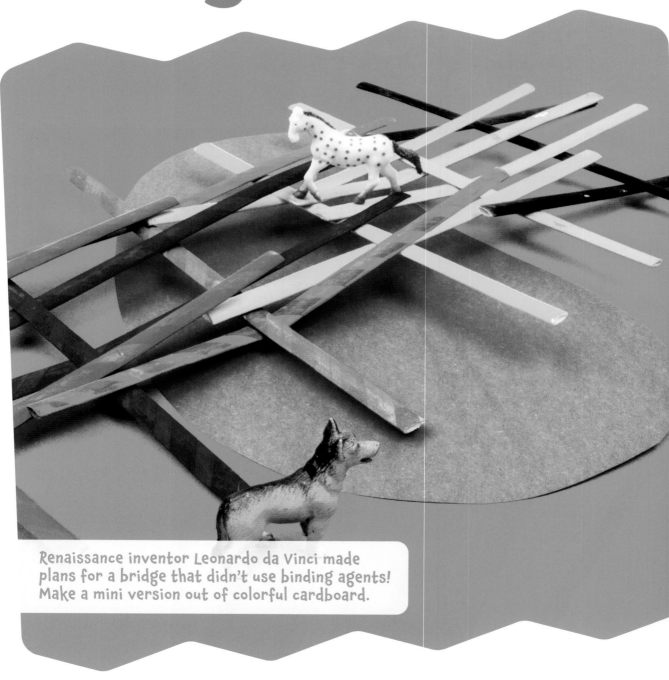

Renaissance inventor Leonardo da Vinci made plans for a bridge that didn't use binding agents! Make a mini version out of colorful cardboard.

Materials:

18 paper straws; ruler; paint; paintbrushes; items with different weights, such as a dry sponge, small toys, or a box of crayons; chenille stems (optional)

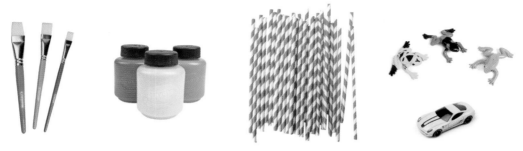

1. Flatten the straws by pinching them and then sliding a ruler across them.

2. Paint the straws. Make three of each color: red, blue, green, yellow, orange, and black. Let the paint dry.

Project continued on next page.

3 Lay a blue straw down vertically. Place two red straws horizontally with their ends lying on the blue straw.

4 Lay the third red straw vertically across the horizontal red straws. The four straws should form a hashtag shape.

5 Carefully slide the two remaining blue straws horizontally under the vertical blue straw. Extend these blue straws until their ends rest on top of the vertical red straw. You should notice the straws lift off your work surface a bit.

6 Slide a green straw vertically under the horizontal blue straws.

7 Slide the other two green straws horizontally under the vertical green straw. Rest the ends of these green straws on top of the vertical blue straw.

8 Place two yellow straws horizontally with their ends on the vertical green straw. The yellow straws should lie between the horizontal blue and green straws.

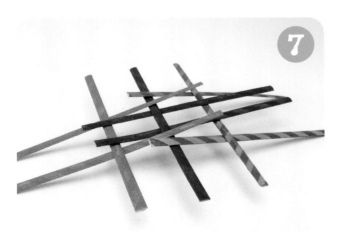

9 Place the third yellow straw vertically across the two yellow straws. Tuck its ends under the horizontal green straws.

10 Slide an orange straw vertically under the horizontal yellow straws.

11 Slide the other two orange straws horizontally under the center of the vertical orange straw. Rest their ends on the vertical yellow straw.

12 Slide one black straw vertically under the horizontal orange straws.

13 Slide the other two black straws horizontally under the vertical black straw near each end. Rest their ends on the vertical orange straw.

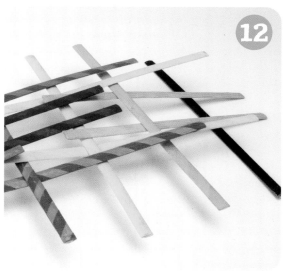

14 Your bridge is complete! Test it by setting small household items of different weights on it. Does the bridge hold up? If not, think about what happened. Did any ends come loose and need to be reset? Would a material other than paper straws make a sturdier bridge?

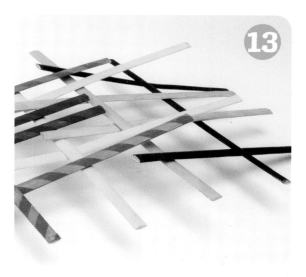

MAKER REMIX!
Mosaic Puzzle

In the Mosaic Puzzle activity on page 12, you created a colorful puzzle from geometric shapes. How else could you use these mosaic pieces? Here are some ideas:

- Try fitting the tiles together to form letters, numbers, or other recognizable shapes.

- Use the mosaic tiles to build a tower, bridge, or other 3D structure. Decide whether you will stack the tiles or connect them with a binding agent such as clay or glue.

- Think about how the shoebox lid could serve as more than just a base for a puzzle. Can the lid be cut up to make thinner mosaic tiles to add to a structure? Could the lid be cut into spikes, legs, or other shapes and glued to the tiles to make mini creatures?

Is it easier or more difficult to fit the mosaic tiles together in a flat pattern or a 3D pattern? Why do you think this is?

GLOSSARY

dense: having molecules that are packed tightly together

discipline: an area of study

engineering: the science of designing and building complicated products, machines, systems, or structures

geometric: made up of points, lines, and angles

horizontally: positioned or moving in a manner that is side to side rather than up and down

mediums: materials or methods used by artists

nonpolar: not having a strong positive or negative electric charge

polar: having a strong positive or negative electric charge

randomly: without a regular plan or pattern

3D: having width, depth, and height

vertically: positioned or moving up and down rather than side to side

vibrate: to move back and forth in tiny, quick movements

LEARN MORE

Crayola: Create It Yourself—DIY Ring Toss
https://www.crayola.com/crafts/diy-ring-toss-craft/

Felix, Rebecca. *Crayola Super Easy Crafts*. Minneapolis: Lerner Publications, 2019.

Halls, Kelly Milner. *Simple Science Projects*. Vero Beach, FL: Rourke Educational Media, 2019.

NASA Science—Space Place: Explore Earth and Space!
https://spaceplace.nasa.gov/

National Geographic Kids—Science Lab
https://kids.nationalgeographic.com/explore/science/science-lab/

Tripp, Karyn. *Math Art and Drawing Games for Kids: Fun Art Projects to Build Amazing Math Skills*. Beverly, MA: Quarry Books, 2019.

WNYC Studios—Radiolab for Kids
https://www.wnycstudios.org/podcasts/radiolab-kids

INDEX

PHOTO ACKNOWLEDGMENTS

The images in this book are used with the permission of: © Morrowind/Shutterstock Images, p. 4 (STEM symbols); © Travelpixs/Shutterstock Images, p. 4 (boy painting); © LightField Studios/Shutterstock Images, p. 5 (girl crafting); Veronica Thompson, pp. 6 (stormy sea beauty), 7 (step photos); © Marcin Perkowski/Shutterstock Images, p. 12 (rolling pin); © MarkoBabii/Shutterstock Images, p. 18. All other images are © Mighty Media, Inc.

Cover Photos: © Mighty Media, Inc.; Veronica Thompson (top right)